T0113037

FLAK JACKET

Some of these poems have previously appeared in print:

Open Wound, *Poems Twofold: A Moncton Collection*, Trans. by Georgette Leblanc and Drew Lavigne, 2024.
Our Giant; My Grave Marker, *Prairie Fire*, 2024.
For Susan Musgrave; Prom Dress; Mimesis; Pain Threshold; Performance Art, *The Sandy River Review*, 2023.
The Last Treatment, *Queen's Quarterly*, 2023.
Hot Spoons, *Queen's Quarterly*, 2022.
The Dying of the Light, *Prairie Fire*, 2022.
Paradise Lost, *The Dalhousie Review*, 2022.
My Grave Marker; Mimesis, *The Nashwaak Review*, 2022.
Toy Store, *Queen's Quarterly*, Spring 2021.
Mrs. Dryned's Rose Garden, *Sanctuary: Coote's Paradise Writers Anthology, Vol. 3*, 2021.
Open Wound, *As You Were: The Military Review, Vol. 12*, Spring 2020.
Work Boots; streetwise poet; and Flak Jacket, *Sanctuary: Coote's Paradise Writers Anthology, Vol 2*, 2020.
The Canonization of Stan Rogers, *Graviṭas, Vol. 19. Issue 2*, Spring 2020.
Jerusalem's Ridge 1996: Canadian Forces Base Gagetown; and Coyotes, *Sanctuary: Coote's Paradise Writers Anthology, Vol. 1*, 2019.
Loss, *The Antigonish Review, Vol. 49, No 196*, Winter 2019.
Driving Lisa to Drug Rehab, *Prairie Fire, Vol 40, No 3*, Spring 2019.
The History of the Monad, *Off the Coast*, Winter 2018.
Cité Soleil, *Queen's Quarterly*, Winter 2018.

Several poems appeared in the Pub House Books 2019 Chapbook Prize publication *Trigger Fingers*.

FLAK JACKET

Poems

GERALD ARTHUR MOORE

CANADA

Cover photo—Vince Swayles "Barn Fire in Southern Ontario"
Cover design—Blake Morin, blakemichelmorin.com

Library and Archives Canada Cataloguing in Publication

Title: Flak jacket : poems / Gerald Arthur Moore.

Names: Moore, Gerald Arthur, 1972- author.

Identifiers: Canadiana 20230577857 | ISBN 9781989689639 (softcover)

Subjects: LCGFT: Poetry.

Classification: LCC PS8626.O5937 F53 2024 | DDC C811/.6—dc23

Printed and bound in Canada on 100% recycled paper.

Now Or Never Publishing
901, 163 Street
Surrey, British Columbia
Canada V4A 9T8

nonpublishing.com
Fighting Words.

We gratefully acknowledge the support of the Canada Council for the Arts
and the British Columbia Arts Council for our publishing program.

For Corrine May

TABLE OF CONTENTS

ANCASTER

THE OUBLIETTE

CHILDHOOD

SCHOOL

HAITI

POSTCARDS FROM IRELAND AND ENGLAND

THE EAST COAST POETS HAVE GONE AWOL

Ancaster

Toy Store

"Harry Bennet lived here
before the toy store;
now he's over there," Dad said,
thumbing toward the graveyard.
Neumann's Toys housed
petrified pink and orange rabbit's feet,
kites with wide bloodshot eyes—
peering madmen,
seductive stick candy soliciting
by the register, scarlet paper ribbon
punctuated with black dots,
spooled through and under
the hammer of my first cap-gun,
quickly took up incautious
trigger-guard twirling.

Constable Bennet
once arrested my father
for calling him a buxom bastard.
Nine years old at the time of his
criminality, vanished through
narrow hedgerow gap, taunting
from veil of hawthorn.
A fortnight later, caught my father
by the ear,
took him to Tommy Beech's Garage,
asked to borrow a car
supposedly to drive his prisoner—
now on tip toes,
down the Niagara Escarpment
to Barton Street Jail in Hamilton.
Tommy played along, *"How long will he*
serve in the clink?"
"Nine or ten years, I'd say, Tommy,
if he behaves."

Lightning storm, years later, took
his pistol, in the flashing *strobos* of
chaos and shot the Anglican church
to death. Must have been mad at God.
If you look with binoculars
the pock marks are there today,
resting craters in belfry limestone,
five rounds into block façade;
then went inside, sat down,
spun the cylinder of his .38,
like the empty hexagonal
wax cells of honeycomb,
a golden round passing
the gun-blue breech chamber,
a circling reflector
clicking like our bicycle wheels.

The Dying of the Light

Our village streetlamps were governed
by a solitary switch, the Prime Mover

of light housed inside a wood box, ten
feet up a lamp pole in the shade

of an old growth chestnut tree that
competed with the Anglican steeple.

My scallywag father used a branch
to trip that switch and turn the village

core dark. A padlock was added to the box.
On rare occasions, it was left unlatched

for him to shimmy the steel pole and claim
another victory.

That tree, whose leaves were like fans,
bore witness, and whose pungent durian

husks, were perfume. Further on this last
walk home, past the proudly polished

brass bell of the fire station, a flat roof
we climbed upon to shoot marbles from

slingshots, to the post office and printer,
the cenotaph, where so many old

village names are written in bronze relief,
whose youth seems remarkable now that

I am old. The juglone from a black walnut,
stained our hands and shoes, we'd step

on the hulls with heel; eviscerate them
free, then collect in a pail.

Further down this memory, a great
heave of lilacs, on to Mrs. Brown's roses,

that I gave away each day to the girl I
walked home, when they were out of reach

I'd hop pristine pickets, careful not to touch
the back of each heavily greased slat.

Everything has a history that points to a
cemetery, where all the stories are whispers.

Every main street was something that
it no longer is, and if that makes you despair

you are forgetting to be grateful for the
numbered walks on homeward

roads, roads that seemed to also point at
forever, a forever you can still smell,

when you amble down the carefully counted
sidewalk squares to the pole that was,

climb one last time, up, up joyously, reach
up laughing to extinguish the light.

Paradise Lost

My binder-twine blisters
are trophies that bleed.

Not only have I been keeping up all
day long, at fourteen I've outworked

every man below; at the supper table
I'll be seated like an apostle.

The wagon arrives like a great ark
birthing sun-warm rectangular bales,

tractor generator spinning, ramped
conveyor's metal teeth riding up track

to yawning hay shoals, laid like
terracotta tiles stacked to the rafters.

Below, men spitting cheeks
of tobacco over each golden offering

ascending Jacob's Ladder.
Was this where I became a man?

Father is wiping his forehead with
a Co-op hat, looking up, smiling.

Under the gambrel, the mow pulsing
heat like a forge,

working from our knees, breathing dust,
dripping dirt, blowing snot;

crepuscular sunset rays capture
hayloft effluent and chaff;

careful now, the rafter-nests are close,
I've already been stung twice,

I knock a wasp's nest, hear it thump down
like the decollation of John the Baptist,

start up like a pull engine— it's every
man for himself.

Slide down the elevator on the inside
ankles of my boots,

driven from Paradise by the swarming
seraphim, fear of Michael's spear,

crawling over bales on their way
to ascension as I am cast out.

Mrs. Dryned's Rose Garden

Midsummer with the untutored
landscape crew for colonial estates,

we were shapeless unwashed workers
with Dutch hoes, scraping metallic

scissor rhythm of hand shears,
manicuring Edenic vistas, trimming

for croquet. Four massive flower beds
open like folio pages or a painted

illumination from The Book of Kells,
a thriving palette of roses—

Demask, Multiflora, Mister Lincoln's
tea, society gardens for sun dress parties,

wicker hats for shade, Pimm's cup
or lemonade, dry gin, scones, clotted crème.

The groundhogs that summer
were prolific in their lovemaking,

Mrs. Dryned hated them
almost as much as she hated us.

My job, at fourteen, was to
skulk from under the ancient pine,

elbow-cradling a bolt action .22
Cooey, with orders to shoot anything

that moved. That summer I killed only
one, Mrs. Dryned heard the report,

she envisioned a slaughter,
and that was enough.

Friends

When Raymond Cantin escaped, we
wondered if he would slip from shadows,

step from vast hazy distances of childhood.
"He'll likely come to the shop."

Years earlier Dad created odd jobs for
Raymond, sanding carts, sweeping sawdust,

compiling cigarette dog ends. Later he
learned bandsaw and blow torch.

We were counting silos on the long drive
to Tillsonberg for milled drop heel

jog-cart shafts, hand smooth Canadian
ash. Raymond was tending the shop

when a horseman dropped in, he followed
that man like race barn stink,

asked why we left our business unlocked.
"The only people who come in here

are my friends." The next day, missing tools
appeared under the workbench.

I gave him sass, once. He pointed and pulled
a composite bow, arrow's omphalos, into a

vanishing point, upsloping cylindrical
corridor, fletcher's feathers clenched in shaking

fist—murderous eyes. Don't know if it was
nocked. Didn't tell anyone.

His cockroach crawl, from courthouse
through air duct over King Street

was newsworthy. Reporters pondered how
Raymond obtained a handcuff key,

looked so young, those fingers now pinching
their numbered placard for his thug-shot.

"Unscrew the porch light, unlatch the slide
door, leave a hundred dollars

in the Swear Jar." And a note,
"For our friend."

SAUGEEN ARROWHEAD

The first one I found while
fishing for wood turtles in a watering
hole; it fought hard, but we tugged
that sacred creature streamside;
always turned toward water;
some type of ancient internal compass,
paddled and hissed, drove its claws
into mud to get back.

There, on an oblique angle, it lay
for centuries in sedimentary strata—
a Saugeen chert, edged like an aspen leaf,
chipped by a perfectionist.
A ferric stained imprint in the clay relief
when it slid out, intact.

I heard the voice, and listened.
Released our turtle—
watched her glide down
to the obfuscation of the warm pool.

Fields of goldenrod—paved over,
cattail edges of winding streams—
gone now.
Marshes drained; woodlands bulldozed;
anaemic tin-trimmed houses, sculpted
cedar hedges, interlocking driveway
patterns slant to ditches,
to mighty cisterns;
water is piped off million-dollar
properties down the escarpment
to Hamilton.

My father says they gutted beauty.
He can't see the irony of the arrowhead
or understand the death of our turtle.
Sometimes I hold the stem, run my
finger across the excurvate blade,
gently on the basal edge, and wait
for her to speak again.

Coyotes

Enticed by fresh afterbirth, they infiltrate the barn,
skitter of claws down the manure chute,

dragged that crying calf from her mother
before it could even stand;

like King David's soldiers skulking into the fortified city
through Hezekiah's cistern,

glinting teeth were smiling swords,
oil-stoned edges, Masonic pledges, unspoken words.

Years ago, a shortcut from the old field cemetery
saw my father cross through tangled overgrowth,

a riot of thorns, erratic hazel scourged;
punctured his palms, speared his side, held his arms,

until he sank to the smooth undulation of a rabbit trail,
crawled out like a soldier through coils of razor wire;

the offended tricksters followed him home that night;
left their scat on his doorstep.

After their threat we kept a lame foal in the barn,
and a good thing too,

the next morning there were seven, laying in defilade
behind a berm, at the bottleneck by the paddock gate;

their knackers yard. Turkey vultures, anticipating the kill,
were already flying in their infinite vortices.

Fork Bracelets

tin dinner forks
bent around
        her thin wrists,
renegade jewelry,
        tattered jeans,
a riot of red hair,

a riot of long red hair,
the tolerance to listen
to my three chord
approximations of
Tom Petty songs,
        took the middle seat
of the pickup truck
even when we were
alone;

        pulled
off bottlecaps with
those strange bracelets,

she'd plot the
roadmap of infinite
possibilities,

        borrow
identities like t-shirts,
borrowed indefinitely,
as if dreams were
clothes.
        Here, try this
poet shirt, what about
an English major,
teacher's jacket,

herringbone with elbow
patches,
   a satchel
to travel the world,

fork bracelets
and a rainbow belt,
tattered jeans,
a riot of red hair,
she'd whisper sing
Free Fallin',
      already
a champion of the
underdog and a patron
of the arts.

Running from Johnny Law

Sulphur Springs was an old friend;
each handhold of that road, known,

with her slalom run of knotted turns,
every footpath and fence, familiar.

Reckless teenage speed,
crested over one hill past an OPP;

flew, literally, none of the
wheels were touching.

Cruiser lights spun-on like fireworks in the rearview.
Hammered the gas-pedal like I was stepping on a shovel,

perhaps the most impetuous decision of my life.
Tapped off the headlights and drove;

taillights fading, wheels squealing protestations
with each turn, tailgate sparks against the inverse slope;

cascade of stars, a waxing gibbous moon
dangling like a plump peach on a low branch,

mileage clicking fast, past St. Andrew's cemetery;
hit Wilson Street and let 'er rip,

full tilt, gear-shift smacking in its skirt,
engine winding up; jumped curbstones

behind Glendale Motors, bashed through a hedgerow
across a yard, skidded home under the black chestnut.

Shut it down; the red-hot block twitching
as she rested in the dew of fresh cut lawn;

fragrant lilacs and mown grass;
soon crickets resumed their choir song,

until sirens came. One, two, three—their voices
rising then falling, fading, toward the QEW.

Closed the truck door. Hot metallic clicks,
six-cylinders complained of being driven too hard.

The single glowing ember of my father's cigarette
on the back veranda.

WORK BOOTS

At the first stoplight
there was a sharp honk
from behind. A complaint?

Bedamned, I flipped the bird,
gave it a little up and down,
waggled it for emphasis;

then slowly accelerated away,
in full control, mysterious.

He followed, waving to get
my attention, then hoisted
a fascist salute.

Cranked the window down,
pointed two fingers at my throat
like a snake bite,
made wide eyes;
screamed *blaaaaaah*
hanging my tongue
like a thirsty gargoyle.

Parked in the shade.
Breathed. Prepared for
a long-armed day
of laying brick;
circular stone saws,
powder gray stone dust snot.

A temporary crown,
precariously perched atop
the old Dodge's cab;
empty work boots,
pinched together, ankles
hugging my metal lunchbox
like strange bookends.

Meat Horses

Clopped rhythmical, through
cloistered stalls,
shoulder to shoulder,
fingers looped
through gritty halter rings.

Knocked Jonogold apples
off the upper branches
with a stick,
filled his hat, let them
feed, went forehead
to forehead with each
warm animal
for a
still
moment,
then stepped back,
raised his arm.

Higher on their head
than cattle,
down through the brainstem,
collapsing over each
other,
the bay twitching,
automatic running,
jagged and abbreviated
seizures,
then a slow contraction
like a burning leaf.

Diesel meat-truck slunk
like a rocket launcher,
bucket lowered, chain winch,
its slow tongue
lapping them up
for the knacker's yard.

My father's vision
is vivid, his dementia
allows these brief
returns, and just as often
they're a mess of regret.

DRINKING BUDDIES

Shared her stall, pressed
against plywood, slept

in shavings, barn perfume,
without ever getting stepped

on by shuffling hooves,
poured stubbies through

waggling lips, frothing
over lolling tongue,

forehead star, human eyes,
that chestnut would smile.

Sunset Lee M could drink
after a race,

impetuous driver gave her
haunch a heavy whipping,

Gerald tore it from fist,
tossed it over the rail,

into the grandstand as if
pulling a sapling,

wept into calloused hands
when she was claimed,

removed familiar halter,
added stiff snaffle bridle,

drove their empty trailer
home, then sobered up.

My father's shovel

Desiccating tomatoes, gray withered stalks,
leprosy elbows bent like my father curving

into himself. Crepuscular rays blazing
through dripping branches, self-pruning poplars

dropping chaff that my boy offers our bonfire,
transforming the lifeless to cinder and ashes.

Morning reaches with pulsing arms of warmth,
when I see spectacular silver lines pulled taught

above leaf litter, thousands of spider webs,
interwoven strands, sunshine on dew lines

appear like cracked windshields when I bend
to pull the last ragged plant of the season,

rattle the rootball, knock the final gasp of dirt
free against my father's shovel.

Our Giant
for Pete Middleton

Drill limestone chambers,
rainwater inundations, wait
for winter expansion to split
blocks, sell to stone masons,
quarried wagonloads up the
escarpment to The Village.

Made his own swish, used
booze barrels refilled with
boil, sugared, leach whiskey
from slats, super ferment to
twenty percent, chase with
dandelion wine, tasted like
sileage.

Nana would soap his hair
once a year, sink-washing,
hand over hand, bucket water
slurry, straight razor sculpture,
slowly touched his smooth
chin with aftershave, kissed
his forehead, he would blush
like sunrise.

Wearing a paper crown at
Christmastide, pint bottles
were small in his massive
hands, where he'd sit on a
step stool—the only chair
that fit him, a giant's
throne.

Pin up girls smiling
in his corrugated shotgun
shack, small woodstove,
firewood stacks were
careful round mounds,
stone walk with soldier
course, birdsong, star
ceiling, AM radio, and axe.

Trundle up Devil's Elbow
past the Old Mill with
a brace of hare by their ears,
lifelessly staring, broken
necks bobbing,
draped them over porch rail
like dolls for Nana.

When he got sick, there
was no one, in his narrow
bunk he cramped and cried,
discovered inside a week after
laying down for the last time,
crows had stolen his eyes.

GENERATIONS

My grandfather
killed in France
was twenty years
younger than I am now,
his hollow broken skull buried
in the Canadian Cemetery
at Beny Sur Mer,

his name, cradled
in the hands of the Peace
Tower, in bronze on village
cenotaph, resting
on my library card,
running through the
arteries of my son.
I place my hand
on the warmth of my boy's
neck, wonder what delights
and dangers he will face.

Fascists emerge after
every storm, each generation
realizes the metastasis. So we are,
each of us, deeply responsible
for kneeling, as if in prayer,
in the moist garden,
searching by feel for their
haggled stems, then gently
manipulating back and forth
like loose teeth,
to see if they will release
root intact.

Some won't. They
will march from darkness
their boot nails colliding
in rhythm step, pointing
their shaking fingers
in the neo-Kristallnacht
that threatens destruction
without dialogue, whose
only language is violence,
who lust for our blood.

This is why we tend
the undulations after rain,
cull the naked rootcap,
pull—horsetail and fern,
pull—taproot anchorage,
break hands holding down
the weak and downtrodden,
take as many lateral
branches as will come,
lay them exposed,
to bake in the sun.

THE OUBLIETTE

Driving Lisa to Drug Rehab
for Kai Gosling

Hatches battened in the head of the gale,
whitecaps slap, the shoreline is a froth.

Lisa's pasted speech is harbour speed
from the junk she uses,

casually mentions that her septum is corroded;
can push her finger all the way through.

Her boyfriend smashed out the storm-door,
There, a mosaic of broken glass glitters

like the glowing Sargasso's highway to the moon.
Dead-eyed corner-boys swim past,

trailer park sharks, dorsal fins, predatorial
turns, always on their chase.

She snorts a Perc, crushed between two quarters,
to smooth the self-loathing of what she does to score,

to quiet her tormentors waiting in the depths,
twisting gear, cutting nets, breaking oars.

No markers on the big waters, drifting buoys,
immeasurable borderlines;

blood promises evaporate with her body mass,
like tall ships taken by Scylla or Charybdis.

Ninety-six pounds of jagged hipline;
raw nipples that were pounded by storms,

anchor tattoos have pinned down her arms,
a hurricane shoreline littered with wreckage,

the stanchions and beams of her ribcage.
She pulls herself into the car; we cast off

for our long drive, up the coast with wind in our sails.
When we drift off course, wheels hit rumble-strip,

grind warning; I correct, tuck back into
my own lane, missing the Siren's call,

the rocky promontories that cave-in hulls,
the crashing waves, the noisy gulls.

In the rearview mirror, she thinks we don't notice
as she fixes one last time;

impossible to know the damage for sure,
or what's under the waterline.

ALEC

When Alec's pick-up crunched our lane,
the whiskey was eclipsed by the crock

of pickled pears. He was a stippled
old drunk that smelled like gin-piss;

who, on my eighth Halloween, dropped
a bottle of beer in my pillowcase.

Collins Hotel regulars called him a character;
he prophesied like Amos from a barstool,

his children waiting outside for hours.
My father recognized the dark lonely distances

he chose; the empty dreams tossed
from a driver's window,

duds that thumped ditches, brittle glass
offerings that glitter before headlights.

His wife finally left after their kids
emigrated to the edges,

East to Halifax and West to Vancouver,
like bookends.

One lean autumn, Dad bought
Alec's old chesterfield and paid too much.

Mother brooded for a week, then said,
"You know he just drank it."

Found him beat-to-shit out by The Reserve;
his burnt skeletal truck torched in a cornfield;

boot-marks on his forehead, a broken crown,
one eye pendulous from its socket;

reminded me of a tiny naked bird,
excommunicated from the nest.

Open Wound

Yellowing apples underneath low branches
fermenting; attracting deer and honeybees,
further down the clear-cut they're burning;
turning orchards to floodplains,
smoking stumps, slow to disintegrate,
hold their heat for days.

In slow pirouettes of smoke—a mule deer.
Something wrong, the way she shuffles
awkward—unnatural.

Circling the cut, inside
shadowed treeline, careful outstep
creeping—I'm quiet. Upwind, but that fire
is going to cancel out my scent.
Drift deeper, then arc back out to the edge
of my imaginary clover leaf, slowly emerge,
keep the morning sun in her eyes.
That's when I see it.

Just above her wet cambered shoulder—
a concave exit wound like a cereal bowl;
writhing worms periodically fall, tapping
leaf litter like heavy raindrops. The smoke,
keeping cluster flies at bay, meat bees
from feasting. Maggots, at least
are cleaning this old gunshot.
She's near the end.

Slowly lifts her head when she hears;
tired glass eyes; I understand.
Unsling;
and curse the motherfuckers
who left us like this.

Loss

The needle on the turntable stuttered
over *vegemite sandwich*
while the headboard tapped
to their alien grunting.
Within the closet, without sightline,
amidst this strange confusing cadence
my cramped annex flashed
with destructive understanding.

Unable to wait any longer;
her shawl over my face
to filter the naphthalene,
plucked my penis and voided,
mostly into a boot, then puddling
around my bare feet, expanding
like Ebola across the laminate.

They were throwing Molotov cocktails
in Northern Ireland, slow march
hard-eyed balaclava funerals.
Iranian hostages; Union Carbide's
gas cloud—innocence culled;
and Ryan White—Michelangelo's AIDS angel,
amputated from school, thrown overboard
like a sacrifice to Neptune. A sea of fear.
Nuclear; Chernobyl's melting core;
mutually assured oblivion, Cold War,
cowering under desks
imagining *The Day After*.

Winter cornstalks, flotsam friendships,
graveyard etchings, the troubled lines
of my father's face, lost marbles,
dull chisels, even my sister's virginity
seemed to be a lesson in the long
agony of subtraction;
and a warning.

MIMESIS

Sleepy plywood eyelids
of frowning row houses.

A peal of church bells plays The Westminster—
La di da-da, La di da-da.

There she is again, a soup-spill,
cigarette-ash psoriasis,

carries that naked doll,
her plastic effigy, an albatross;

Child Protective Services peeled her fingers
off the doorframe decades ago.

Stovetop ball-hat corner boys, dial-a-dopers,
fentanyl werewolves, hair-trigger stare, pit bull terriers.

A kid in my wife's class says, "Momma works
on Waterloo Street,"

her emaciated legs have the best veins
for shooting-up,

barefoot in cowboy boots, Johns order her to shower
before they start.

These leaning houses need cleaning ladies;
the city's *priority tenements* are distortion mirrors,

blinds pulled on shuttered lives, Christ,
must mean more than Sunday tithes.

Susan Musgrave

free verse for felons,
his girlfriend, a handgun

poet who answered
hotel room doors

barely dressed, bare
breasted, shoulder

holster, checkered
walnut handle

the .357 caressing
the nipple.

your lines were songs
I drank, youthfully

awake, aware of the
possibility of living

as a writer, trespassing
into another life.

STEPHEN REID

tiny holes punched
through café spoons
to deter junkies,
Downtown Eastside
at thirteen,
your slam damaged
arms made nurses cry,

morphine's sleepy
dreamscape, to chasing
dime stacks in the
oubliette of East Hastings,
booty bumps to your
surrogate, a strung out
prostitute trading street
knowledge for H,
cotton fever overdoses,

toward highwire robbery,
taking down heavy scores,
nefarious stopwatches,
armed and garish
disguises, evaporating
ether trail to cover lives,
FBI's most venerated
timekeepers, until your
capture, then became
an escape artist.

twenty-one years
of slow time, clear
headed solitude
to write memoires,
submission to The Great
Musgrave, ignited
the strangest Canadian
literary landscape love
story. later, in *Crowbar*
your confessions offered
a why. why you peeled
back to the dope carnival,

an abyss that spiraled
to that first suave
doctor, pedophile pusher
who hopped you up
at 11. decades later
would cross him again
in the prison infirmary,
he'd ignore you.

conditional release,
a slip, soon slamming
junk again, your last
botched bank job, coke
fueled, shot gunning
to another long bit.

your child
knows her dad through
redacted letters, smudged
window visits, grad photo
taped to a cell wall,
finally, another old
rabbit on parole.

breaching killer
whales swimming
Haida Gwaii's community
inlet. foreshadowing
newspaper obituaries that
would reduce you to
writer, bank robber,
addict.

the last time
I asked which actors
could play Susan Musgrave
and Stephen Reid,
Angelina Jolie, you laughed,
and Eddie Murphy.

ODE ON A MARTINI URN

Initially, they thought they were using an eccentric
teapot for her cinerary urn;

somebody in the family had purchased the silver
vessel at a yard sale, and Kim, they all said,

liked tea. But there was something special about
its stumpy body type, the tiny polished top hat;

more like a canopic jar than something for
Darjeeling.

A blueish-grey ceiling, dirty jean jacket overcast,
pathetic fallacy; slush sliding

down a car windshield, steeping skyline
flowing over us while eulogies evaporated;

reflected in the shoulder of the thing;
then realizing it wasn't a teapot either,

it was a martini shaker! Kimberly, shaken
not stirred. Gearwheels clicked

like a metronome as they lowered her into the
mudscape eternity of moist earthworms

and mushroom spores. This strange tiny platform
dressed like a small marionette stage;

her ashes winched through, *deus ex machina*,
out of sight: *Exeunt.*

A whole life, indifferently resolved;
and it's Happy Hour in the West.

Prom Dress

Lisa was an addict. To everything.
Late shifts as a shooter girl, amplified

tips that transubstantiated to opioids;
she'd scare-up on coke, ascend the ladder

then slide the long snake down
with Perks and Oxys,

take whatever pills were masquerading
as the gospel.

Overdose, heart attack, and then brain dead:
Sunday's Eucharistic cannibals gave

her a baptism before unplugging life support.
There was a lump in my throat the size of Jesus

at the funeral, where she lay
in her prom dress.

Pain Threshold
Inspired by "A Cargo Handler Howls" by Zach Wells

Protest for longer
in the searing fear of tear gas
cannisters, as skirmish lines
get rougher,
for longer than they will,
I will,
suffer.

I can suffer slow death,
months of lassitude,
linen changes,
scores of bedsores,
the rat stench of betrayal
as her body died.

Drink ferric mouthfuls
of failure, abide the endless
attrition of a pandemic,
managing the growing horror,
solitary on the teeter totter,
the milk of truth has turned sour
across the border.

Without sleep for days,
chained forward in dark caves,
downwind from mass graves,
face punched, pommeled,
kicked like a rotten stump,
stagger up—stagger on,
ragged, rippcd kneed, laughing
at the taste of my blood.

I can swallow fear,
cross a valley of dry bones
tripping over despair
in broken ruins,
through bombed cityscape,
listening to sinister whispers
from shadow men.

That I can suffer, endlessly,
is what makes me tougher.

Easy Childhood

Sawdust Perfume

Burnt tree sugars captured in the ledger
of memory, that eternal season

when love was in surplus, when family
dinners were still at our house.

The Rockwell Beaver band saw was
bolted to the shop floor,

with vice grips substituted for a
guide clamp, until last week,

I gave it to a farmer with a knack for old
machines. As we loaded it, I recalled

Dad fashioning blunt claymore swords,
few words exchanged while he worked,

whirring motor, whining woodcuts, blurred
blade slipping through grain, sawdust perfume.

Sawdust on our fingers to pick dew worms
to plunk into trout ponds,

in competition with high stepping robins,
who, when teaching their fledglings,

became mad dive bombers descending,
face whipping with daring wingtip flares.

After musical chairs, trundling rainy
sidewalk squares,

Dad waiting beneath a curtain of willow,
encircled by bursting April crocus, car tires

hissed over wet pavement, windshield tears,
He announced, "Your Aunt Patricia is dead.

It's like she's sleeping. She was—murdered.
Her boyfriend did it. They were drunks."

The next bludgeoned summer, at the band saw,
that descending blur of steel

caught his shirtsleeve, yanking him toward
a thirsting abyss, how quick he was to spin

and wheel, violently ripping free, then
remarked, "So what did ya' learn from this?"

My father made magnificent swords,
spoke few words. I remember

the car lights swinging across wallpaper
between the swaying branches of time,

sleeping with my wooden sword to defend
my family against unknown dangers,

I remember her smirking boyfriend's stare,
ice jingling in whiskey tumblers,

the way Patricia glided so perfectly into
a room, and I remember sawdust perfume.

THE ILIAD

The broken stone walk was
a battleground.
My father and I sat on the stoop,
looking down at the carnage
like Greek gods, with loyalties
and preferences.

I'd sided with the striped ants
whose gold trim made them
more beautiful in my eyes.
They landed a thousand ships
on shores. Dad's hordes were
the native species, Ilium.
My invading Achaeans,
so numerous that we detoured
across the lawn, keeping from the
writhing sea of bedlam.

On the third day fighting had
broken into platoon sized,
wager-worthy conflagrations.
Dad and I started betting nickels.

Dardanoi tactics were
to single out a foe
for group-assault, their victims
dismembered. Loners
eventually snatched, dragged,
pinned down, dispatched.

We admired Odysseus, who had so
much to live for at home, his wife
Penelope, his boy too young to plough,
in every action, distinguished and
sturdy, with his loyal crew;

witnessed Hektor strip Patroclos
of his armour, his incisors tore
thorax from abdomen, took
his head for a prize.

And the rage
of the swift six-footed Achilles
who tracked him down, a revenge
killing, where he humiliated Hektor
by dragging him around the edge
of the sidewalk, from the battlefield
into the wilderness.

It was then,
Ajax lost his mind, the imprint
of violence would bleed his core,
stored like pheromones in the
food trails of memory, and once
you turn on the kill switch, how
do you turn it off?

Poor Ajax,
who's suicide in Salamis
years after the war
still leaves us teary eyed.

Nothing has changed,
old men still send young heroes to fall
on battlefields,
watched over by giants casting wagers,
crouching on the stoop,
over the mad melee of childhood.

VIKING PINECONE

In the Archaeology News I'm astonished that
scientists have unearthed a well-preserved
piece of Ninth-Century Viking poop.
Hearty, as you might expect from a Viking.
I show the picture to my three-year-old son.
He's recently taken to calling his solid waste, pinecones.

"That's a pinecone!" He declares in amazement,
perhaps wondering why, "A great big pinecone!"
I tell him it's from a Ninth-Century Viking.
He says, "It's a great big Ninth-Century Viking pinecone."
And I think, one day, he could be excavating a square;
shaving at a layer like Kathleen Kenyon.
Studying stratigraphy, dusting with a small brush
for potsherds, troweling, unearthing coprolites,
to realize our bleak metaphysical hollow;

we are all destined for the same ossuary, desiccating
in the bone box of time after our poem is recited
—for a brief reprieve from the contingent;
offering us something we don't have
in life—a beginning and an end.

Incident at Northrop Frye Elementary School

While flutter kicking off
snow pants

Finley also shucked
his bottoms.

Arrived at kindergarten class
in tighty-whiteys,

socks, indoor shoes, and striped
jacket like a deranged colonel,

Mrs. O'Brian asked where
the lower half

of his track suit went.
He looked surprised,

"Papa," he said, "must have forgotten
to put them on me."

Describe a Perfect Day, Finley's Response (Age 4)

Pickles,

fireworks,

and a bridge troll.

Walking to the plate—bases loaded

Genuflecting umpire, purifying the plate;
precious pentagon unearthed
like an ancient cuneiform tablet.
Batter's boxes are suggestions at this point.
In the contemplative of the on-deck circle,
studying their pitcher
who throws four consecutive balls;
the last three—splitters.

Calibrated now, bases—pregnant;
he'll want to get on top of this count.
The fastball—imminent;

I will crowd, scrape the back of the box
for a foothold, open my hips like a lever...

The sound I *felt* was wet and bone.

Opened like a rusty faucet,
mouth copious—ferric inundation;
slippery eel trying to drown me,
rolling over; twisting ribbons pour,
thirsting dirt laps puddling lakes,
kaleidoscope disorientation,
distant air raid siren—my nose—
emigrated to left cheekbone.

Turns out the bat-boy—one of those jangly
kids, needed to be in constant motion,
so, they let him retrieve the sticks.
Unilaterally decided to take a practice
swing as he ambled, distracted—
toward the dugout.

Quintessential truth;
anticipation often becomes nothing,
no way to know for certain—
what is coming.

Auger

Car brakes,

squealing dog,

as real as bone cancer

or a 3am doorbell,

an unwanted phone call,

we are all force fed from

the Tree of Forbidden Knowledge,

creaking door hinges,

grain bins where

children are playing,

whose laughter disappears,

spiraling abyss,

a tiny yelp into an air pocket,

before their father

starts the auger.

The bone breaking auger,

spinning grist,

the impossible

anchor of grief,

        like the albatross

                of a lonely

loaded shotgun,

        shoulder slung,

                the exhilaration

his first time,

        the accidental discharge

                punching a hole through

his sister's ski jacket,

        a tuft of feathers

                the unholy report echoes,

headlines and deadlines,

        breaking news,

                Russian war crimes,

poet's slant rhyme,

        our whispered prayers

                at bedtime,

fossil fuel pollution,

        climate change solutions,

                another school shooting,

for if they die before I wake.

School

J IS MY ORIGIN STORY

Like a shorebird with a mussel shell,
in a way that happens in high school;

before a violent drop to breakwater rocks,
the soft exposure of flesh, harvesting of meat.

Secret spies, slipping into equipment room solitude
behind a blooming bin of lacrosse sticks,

the echo drum-percussion of basketballs,
a squeaking myriad of stops and starts.

Through that wardrobe you took me to Narnia's
limitless wonder, on bald tires over highway miles

that summer. One night, pulled over by the OPP speeding;
I was wearing a Grateful Dead tie-dye t-shirt, you were topless,

arms folded in faux modestly. He offered the citation;
a bravo-smile underling his moustache.

Spent a patient afternoon drinking longnecks
and scarifying my back with the letter J, in hickeys.

Now, thumb smudged in a yearbook, you are reclining
across the tank of a motorcycle like a half note rest,

the caesura of our lives, where we paused together,
rolled down backroads, stoned inside stadiums,

skipped stones on the Great Lakes, skipped classes,
found the corners of cornfields, you were bread, and I, molasses.

Even then, the cows were already lying down in the fields,
dark clouds calling from the distance.

PERFORMANCE ART

tailpipes
dripping gonorrhea,
three paddy wagons
lined up like grave markers,
someone sitting curbside,
handcuffed,
so I ate our mushrooms.

cellophane tied in a knot,
swallowed that too.
spinning watch hands,
felt my body thermostat
spike.
drug dogs grinned.
I winked back.

through their checkpoint,
found a watermelon stand,
my head, now on fire;
used a flick knife to make
a helmet,
gouged out handfuls;
tender pink flesh,
wore it.
giant hogweed rose from
the ditches like
Day of the Triffids,
a caliphate of cow parsnip,

swarming honeybees
and hornets
arrived to worship,
a misunderstanding,
they came in waves
of confusion, panic,
suicide attackers
en masse.

my face became
a Picasso.

STREETWISE POET

she lives by herself,
works full-time hours,

thighs with tattoos of
wormwood flowers,

usually misses
last class on Mondays,

under the overpass
with junkies and runaways;

glass bus stop shelter,
verse on triptych,

English class poetry
written with lipstick;

she knows how to keep
the weirdos at bay,

flashing butterfly,
can of pepper-spray;

Augustine's *Confessions*,
the stealing of pears,

resting bitch face,
Egyptian kohl stare.

Mushrukit משרוקית
for Zohar and Nir El

Noam's presence in a classroom was
that of a coyote on the other side of
a chain link fence, he'd look through
the diamond gaps, interpret your body
language for signs of weakness,
or perhaps permission.

Tragically late for his final exam;
went partying in the woods, was a
no show. Searching the most likely haunts,
evidence of bicycle trails and foot traffic
through morning dew. A body-print
relief in newly mown field where
someone had slept or died.

Blew my whistle, shouted his name.
He crawled from a tent like Gollum,
dragging from drink, jogged to school
to write his exam in progress
and passed. That Hanukkah he gave
me a silver whistle, his name engraved
on the barrel, his grin profound, eyes
were deep pools of contagious laughter.

This year I'll sing his name, then
blow it seven times, like a trumpet.

DAVID'S STAR

Merry pranksters, subject to
rear-pulling gravity, filled the
caterpillar back rows
like tail gunners.
Mr. Chester's spectacles were
shot glasses, thick as thumbs:
even with, he could only see
the keen nosed first-desk children.

Shop-class:
five lines of five chairs;
heavy box and pan brake
for folding sheet-metal; a lathe
spinning on its axis;
the mangled corkboard
had experienced so much violence
it looked like an axe throwing target.

Our shuriken were dangerous,
we'd carefully grinded away burrs
from tin-snip cat ears. David's were
the most ambitious, huge six tined
affairs—his father was superintendent
of Wentworth County schools.
When retrieving a thrown star
was hit, dead-centre-forehead.
The point bent on impact,
hooked into his skull like
a tin talon,

blood streamed,
lips a–scream
in comic profile
past doorway gawkers.
David, weak–kneed
supported on either side
by teachers,
elbows linked like protestors,
like the Magi,
following
a shining star.

THE SCHOOL

Science lab skeletal snakes
animated,
supernaturally venomous,
striking a teen's small
breast,

belt sander's torn tread
spun up and claimed an
eyeball,

ice weight whiteout
too much for the gymnasium
roof, crumpled like a garbage
lid, fell in great I-beam,
bent rebar, cinderblock heaps;
ball hockey teams
below, shirts and skins,
most killed by debris,
the rest froze.

An executioner stood
with his axe, silent,
they were brought
to the stage;
students, Principal,
Vice Principal,
who kneeled with
their faces turned
toward the crowd;
when their heads fell
their expressions changed.

Mr. Buckle taught grade
eight English:
these were the stories
he wrote—
in between canoodling
the Home Ec teacher
and smoke breaks.

CURRENTLY FAILING PHYSICS

Edgy kid asks his teacher
what he needs to do to pass Physics;
Teacher doesn't miss a beat,
"Invent a time machine."

*What will you do if I invent a
time machine?   Will I get an A?*

Nope, I'll kill you, and take it
back to 1999. I'll go to Florida
and tell Ralph Nader I'm from
the future. He'll listen. He must—
he's a smart guy. I'll come loaded with
proof that only a time traveller
could have. When he finally believes,
he'll come back with me—today.

Al Gore will win the Florida recount;
our fragile earth will be saved.
Good pieces will fall together,
and if buildings still fall that September,
there won't be an incommensurate
War on Terror, no second Iraq War,
no racist resurgence,
no Trump.

So much rides on this one kid,
currently failing Physics.

THE STRAP

I

The strap hung behind her academic gown
like a flat licorice tail, about the width of a cow tongue.

Mrs. Lowry, the Vice Principal, was given the duty
of carrying out my punishment—should it come.

She was my first love. Everything she did was perfect.
Her broom straw hair captured light, the fur

on her arms was like the hide of a giraffe. I made
excuses to conference at her desk;

frankincense radiating from her skin. Intentionally
misspelled *February* so I'd have to write out

my mistakes again and again.
"Now, use it in a sentence."

These sentences blushed: "In *February*, I noticed
Mrs. Lowry looked pretty in her sea blue dress."

II

A trio of fist fights during recess, upper cuts that split chins,
a schoolyard palooka's hat trick: I was Tiger Williams.

Sent home with a terrifyingly-pink envelope—
Rosencrantz and Guildenstern's sealed scroll—

their permission slip, authorizing a dollop
of corporal punishment.

III

This was a time when parents were asked for consent
to have their child flogged. In this strange liminality, I existed,

with the labia-pink letter. Reacting to my tears, Mom refused;
you can always count on moms. Dad barely read it and signed.

At sunset, in the orchard, he explained the inevitability
of pain; said never run from fears or bears;

that an honest life is plumb, level, and square;
to remember that our lies leave scars;

to look both ways for cars—
as we ate plums and pears.

IV

That endless night, dreary and sleepless
when Whiskey-sour Jack arrived;

like Cannon Scott who stays up with the condemned
before his march to the execution pole.

Jack cradled my head, offered advice,
"When Mrs. Lowry gives you the strap, don't cry.

Promise you'll look her dead in the eye, and after,
kiss her on the cheek like Judas."

V

Nobody, it seemed, had ever signed one of those letters.
Mrs. Lowry, unsure, took the heavy tongue down,

removed her *Claddah* ring; it sang with the hardwood.
Placed her warm hand over my wrist,

hand supine, leaning together,
intimately woven, my palm surrendered.

The strap hissed through dead air.
We still wonder how hard she laid the switch,

memory is imperfect; I don't recall any pain
or the number; can still feel the effort to staunch tears,

the humiliation and bitter realization
that our Beatrice was branding my virgin hand.

Silent tears rising like Thermopylae springs,
I regret not being more like Leonidas.

VI

It ended. I whispered inaudibly. She leaned down
when *I did it*; softly pressed my lips to her cherubim face.

The stoicism shattered; she became a crest gate—
as if wounded, shoulders-shaking;

"*I'm so sorry*," she confessed.
"*Please* forgive me."

Then dried my cheeks with her long soft hair.
I wondered if Whiskey-sour Jack was a prophet.

VII

What was normal only yesterday
seems appalling today. When Mrs. Lowry died

we gave her casket the strap, buried her
with *that* anachronism, forgave every sin and offense,

perfumed her body
with myrrh and frankincense.

HAITI

CITÉ SOLEIL
for Rich Mears, who survived

Women pass with their wicker crowns
of clean clothes, laughter is a ripe fruit.

Morning inhales, mists evaporate uphill
toward the ramshackle sounds of a beginning.

Dew-wet barefoot children, school bound;
so different from the days after the earthquake.

That's what I'm thinking, dozing at the wheel
when the passenger door is thrown open.

Lifts up his shirt, shows the taped grip,
the pistol tucked into his waistline

like a vainglorious question mark. A book is
slammed down in my brain. Must have

been a starter pistol; until the blood puddles the seat.
There is a small pea sized hole in the driver's door,

cramping in my leg, and I feel a cloud of shock
darkening like a blanket draped over my head.

The man who drove to the Médecins Sans Frontières
tent didn't know how to drive standard.

Later, I called my phone and spoke to the shooter.
He seemed genuinely relieved that I was alive

and promised to throw the twenty-two
into the Artibonite River,

where the queens of Haiti
are doing their laundry.

Reverse Osmosis

They're making massive pillars
of ice, slowly melting, insulated
under mounds of rice. Outside
the factory, children lay
in a shallow channel
where water runs.

Nick picks up a child sick with
Cholera, jaundice eyes, her tiny
organs failing. These kids
are balancing on the edge of the
razor. Nick begins to place them
on the truck. There is nowhere
to go, so I collect her,
cradle carry like she's my child,
return her to the cool muck, wet
her lips with my canteen to feel
better about leaving, but she is
too sick to drink.

We drive away
from children in a sluice ditch.
On the road move to Port-
au-Prince, with the sun setting
into Le Canal de Saint-Marc,
we get fucked up on vodka
and Gatorade.

POSTCARDS FROM IRELAND AND ENGLAND

A PAUSE ON A SNOWY EVENING BEFORE VENTURING TO THE TURF TAVERN

for Steve Hay

Snow pirouetting the quadrangle,
circumscribing muted footsteps from
the street, wide slow lazy turns like
bathwater, boot nails against bread
loaf cobble between Jesus College
and Exeter. Coral voices shear off
the quiet, a gift, where we pause
in the stained-glass glow.

I'm reminded, by my friend, that
T.E. Lawrence shot the stone wall
across The Turl, his revolver waged
a celebration of noise in the echo
chamber of undergraduate studies.

We're both a little drunk as we
sling our bookbag bandoliers,
mount bicycles like camels
to cross foreign deserts, realize
dangers and choose our battlegrounds.
And Lawrence, fined five pounds
by The Provost of Jesus, not for
lawless sodden gunplay, for noise.
You may fire your pistol with the
peal of bells from Tom Tower,
ringing, but ought to be deathly
quiet, when the choir is singing.

Hidden Guns

Guitar plectrums pinched with trigger fingers;
din conversations disguised in the confessional

of a snug while uilleann pipe bellows elbow pump.
Her snake wood tipper's percussive blur

like a Spitfire propeller upon the spine of a goatskin—
the meridian. Airy voiced seraphim armed with black

pint glasses; secrets unfold through fiddle leads.
Gun-metal eyes, backs to walls will deny flanking,

thirsty wooden planking, scraping chair legs above *them*,
hidden under floorboards, tight shrouds—oily rags,

balaclavas and tri-colour flags. Remembered,
yet unmapped, like the unmarked graves

of fingerless informants, sleeping in Belfast hills—
scattered seeds beneath hedgerows.

Talking with Aemon, silver hair, bowed shoulders,
when I'm snatched and pommelled,

barely touch the floor as I'm hauled into the alley
by muscled brawlers, tattooed forearms and fists,

hard-eyed serious, car reverses in a flood,
back passenger door yawning like a snake.

"Did the army send you here to ask us questions?"
I fast talk, try not to piss, knees surrender,

trembling lips claim that I came to see
the volunteer graves in Milltown.

Reading truth in each rapid breath, my chest
is a bodhrán drum; the longest caesura.... of my life.

When they believe, tears come. Unfed, the snake
becomes taillights. They apologize.

Back inside they slide a Guinness;
my wedding ring taps like a cymbal.

Their barman produces a key to the cemetery gate.
The Falls Road is watching, gaunt murals

of hunger strikers peer from corner row houses.
Pass through the arch into a forest of Celtic crosses,

standing sentries, for centuries. A topiary
of stone crucifixions, old bones, murdered martyrs,

bombers and blanket men—Bobby Sands
with his comrades of Long Kesh, The New Republican

Plot; smooth polished markers like night sky waters;
the murky depths of resistance, and violence.

BIRTHDAY CARDS FOR THE GHOST OF WILLIAM SHAKESPEARE

Our neighbour's landscape orb
was used to break into my car,
a beauty too, the rock not the car,
smooth millennia being polished
by sand and waves,

spent a blink in their English garden
until some scallywag smashed
the passenger window,
stole my ancient leather satchel,
plump with students' work.

Dear Will, did you know
you didn't even spell
your name right, or consistently?
What's with Shak-spear?

Imagine their surprise when
they realize; oh, how
they'll feel ashamed for taking
the great Bard's letters.

Attention: Ghost of Shakespeare,
Your best insults include:
"You rat catcher"
from Romeo & Juliet,
or Twelfth Night's *"Ass Head"*
and your darling,
"Away you three-inch fool"
from Taming.

Care of: The Vicar
Holy Trinity Church,
Stratford-upon-Avon.

And every April to
The Rose & Crown Pub
Charlbury, Oxon.
The spirit poet roams
the Southern Cotswolds,
doom'd for a certain term
to walk the night,
to yellow stone villages
in search of real ale.

Tom, the landlord,
makes sure they
decorate his premises,
folded cards on floating
shelves. Drinkers
give theatrical readings.

Dear Mr. Shakespeare,
happy 455th. Did you really
die on your birthday after
partying with your friends?

Watch out
for the pickled herring.

Şâir, Turkish for Poet

His sweaty thick neck, and chuffing
about how *long* it was taking,
standing cue at the Charlbury kabab stand
after pub. Shouted his filthy slur that
stroked against guard hair, hung
like a chalkboard scrape and pressed
on the invisible place where anger is
conceived.

"Hey," I shouted. "Don't call
my friend that again, or get used to
drinking soup through a straw." I was a
little drunk, but confident enough
I could take this dog for a walk.
Fat Neck told me that Sadat didn't
know, claimed he didn't speak English.
I convinced Neck that if heard again,
I was going to George Chuvalo his face.
Neck became as silent as sweat stains.

Last customer, Sadat wouldn't take my money.
Produced a Turkish to English dictionary,
asked what I did, about my life and family.
At first I looked up soldier, turned to student,
finally settled on *Şâir*—poet. We laughed
brightly together, like a peal of church bells.

MOLLIE DANIEL

On leave, she clenched his dog-tags in her teeth
when they made love; her body was a prayer.

His salvation at Dunkirk was a Padre,
who gave up his seat in a rescue boat,

over the gunnel, waded back to the beachhead
bobbing like a shorebird.

Mollie Daniel, driving diesel on D-day,
towing 400 gallons of holy water.

Greasy tarmac beside the muted planes;
soldiers were shading the back of their hands,

trembling cigarettes, teeth gleamed
like sun-bleached-bones against face-paint,

like the chalk cliffs of Dover paired
with the mudscape of the Channel's low tide.

Fearing capture, they cut their unit flashes off,
the bayoneted bare spots on their shoulders complained silently.

Sutured their badges to her scarf; gifts from boyish ghosts;
the Normandy shoreline accepted their blood sacrifice.

Immigrating to Canada, children in tow, one suitcase;
that olive drab Army scarf was folded like love letters,

hasty goodbyes from nameless strangers, faded emblems,
her talisman, drawn together onto the felt landscape of her youth.

That afternoon in London, his dog-tags in her teeth
when they made love; her body a prayer.

HISTORY OF THE MONAD
for Greg, Michelle, and William

Dull wire-rim eye glasses in a picture frame:

The first time Greg saw his wife, he was wearing
someone else's Bolshevik spectacles,
large wire ovals; Trotsky would have worn them,
they were in the style of revolutionaries.

He borrowed them for a moment,
to be able to see the Eiffel Tower.
Through those lenses she appeared;
emerging like an anthem of truth or a raised fist
and declared the world a better place.

That's it. That's how he saw his Beatrice for the first
time—through a pair of borrowed lenses.
She wasn't atop a steel blue mountain—robe billowing,
or unfurling a tri-colour banner, rather,
she was in the contemplative, looking Heavenward.

The mother of his future child,
at the base, staring up into the omphalos of the truss,
shielding her eyes from the glare of progress's arcing
wrought iron triumph.

Their eyes met in recognition and laughing wonderment
in the great monadology of time and space,
where they oscillated and vibrated in tandem
exulting the most optimistic revolutionary notion—that of
romance, the great climb towards the poetic zenith
of union, into the spire of longing, toward a lifetime
of tomorrows together, like two lenses,
bound in a wire frame.

The East Coast Poets Have Gone AWOL

JERUSALEM'S RIDGE 1996:
CANADIAN FORCES BASE GAGETOWN

Last light was an immolation,
the sky looked like well-worn jeans.

50 cal tracer rounds ricochet upward
like falling stars in reverse.
Blackout road-move, Bombardier Darcy
driving our Iltis, following a glow-stick
taped to a Howitzer barrel,
and a second fixed to its shield—for depth.
Gun tractor drivers wore all the NVGs,
leaving us one pair short.
We adapted.

About an hour later—tumbling
end-over-end like a midway ride.
My rifle, named Lizzie Borden,
had been sleeping on the passenger mirror,
hit *terra firma*, bounced back into the jeep
—then went berserk.

Lizzie Borden became a pinball that was
strangely attracted to Darcy.
RSM Andrews, who had been directly
behind me, was now in the front with us.
Wheels spinning like vinyl records when
our jeep came to a violent halt on roll bars;
the petrol cap had gone AWOL.
Darcy was cursing the Army
like a mortally wounded Mercutio; some
of his face was hanging from Lizzie's front sight
like a dry-cleaning tag. The RSM,
stoic as a Swiss Guardsman,
smirking with an axe, in a torrent felled a tree,
limbed it and levered the jeep upright.

First light was an immolation,
the sky—well-worn jeans.

To LGen. Romeo Dallaire
after "We're Hardcore" by Gord Downie

Dallaire, you've tumbled into this Divine Comedy
with no canto for genocide. Your *contrapasso* is that
of the soothsayers, who walk forever with their
heads on backward.

The metallic scrape of a machete over stone, dragged
lazily against the road, *analepsis* to bloating bodies
pulsing in the tidewater's froth, floating manikins—
like naked Christian statuary bobbing in rivers of blood—
blood muzzled dogs, that unmistakable smell,
meeting *Interahamwe* leaders, their emotionless abyss,
the neutral birdsong at daybreak.

Floating above the narthex of Nyarubuye sanctuary—
Christ with his arms out, ignored
as they pried the metal doors, threw their grenades,
surged through with spears on their mad purge.
School uniforms, folded on dovetail pews
in this public mausoleum. Their dry bones
sorted and stacked.

When radio RTLM cackled with dark instruction
'to cut the tall trees down'—when the voices
of the world were silent, somehow you stayed
and bore witness; defended the stadiums,
your soldiers armed with clipboards.

Mbaye Diagne is one who floats—like that Jesus
above the entrance in Nyarubuye. He could
turn a righteous smile on drunk murderers—
transcend the meanest checkpoints, past thirsting
axes and twisting drills, saving Tutsis by the score;

he was hardcore. Until a mortar attack on a bridge
tore him open like a martyred saint. Without body bags,
you shrouded him in a UN flag and sent him home
to Senegal.

Extremists put out a reward for your head; still,
you moved through Kigali with cavalier confidence,
let on you were deeply offended—thought you should
be going for more. You're hardcore.
You're hardcore.

The Berlin Wall

We sipped homemade schnapps
from jam-jars. Hundreds of miles
in bar-cars. Holding hands like cherry stems
through checkpoints and border crossings.
In all the ways that mattered, Karen
stamped my passport. *La petit mort* in
The Zeemanshuis in Antwerp, we whispered
of our relatives killing each other.

Her father's East Berlin defection—
an underwater escape, with a jerry-rigged
hot water bottle breathing-apparatus.
Café patrons in wait; jumped into the Spree River,
a splashing mass, trading hats and kissing,
hidden in numbers like piping plovers pinwheeling.
Aiming down, unable to pick him out, border guards
were already phrasing their excuses for the Stasi.

Waiting to leave Kraków, atop a train platform
to forever, she passed me a graffiti tattooed rock—
about the size of an apple;
her piece of the Berlin Wall.
Karen accepted that burden, bundled in her pack
through our heady days together—her story
chosen like David's sling-stone
with its killing weight.

CAPTAIN FANTASTIC

Combat issued cold weather long johns,
unexpectantly paired with blackened boots,

deep tread inundated with Bosnian clay,
stainless-steel wash basin for the ceremonial

helmet, as wide as a pith, gun-tape chinstrap,
waffle-scarf-cape completed the ensemble,

the philosopher's stone to a war zone's
monotony, inside the razor-wire, overlapping

arcs of fire; sand-bag bunkers, grey smudged
modular canvas tents, hissing Naphtha lanterns,

into the Officers' Mess; American Army major
gobsmacked, "*What the fuck are you?*"

"*I'm Captain Fantastic.*" Contact, then
a hasty peel-back to barracks,

a quick change to your secret identity.
Regimental Sergeant Major, a pounded

anvil of a man, purposefully striding
across the parade square,

"*You're not in shit Corporal Garland, but if
I ever need Captain Fantastic, he is here*

when I snap my fingers." Like any super-hero,
I suppose.

SUMMER MEMORIES

Othman
had seen one,
nothing lasts long
in the waving heat,
payraan tumbaam
torn from clothesline,
unnatural arms
splayed beneath,
tongue protruding
like a dried eel,
purple pea sized
headwound,
wrists bound
with zap straps.

Bare feet,
quietly from
their village, crossing
fields of saffron flower,
through taller opium
poppy, sticky rivulets
dripping fever dreams.

The slope behind
Hesco barriers,
Asayish
police station,
mud brick walls,
straw binding,

overlooking
the wadi that ran,
a fold
through the entire
valley,
skin wriggling,
sticky flies,
scheming villains
landing on eyes,
staring

into the abyss.
Using a stick to
poke, prod
its bloated belly,
then to school,
privileged
with his rank
of new knowledge,

like the September
I returned from
summer vacation,
whispering
to a gaggle
of grade fours,
astounded
by my understanding
of what I thought
sex was.

GAGETOWN

I don't have any war stories,
just ones from training,

an accident or two, anecdotes
that I recite like poems,

dark comedies, Iltus accident,
AWOL charges, Sarges,

Sergeants with insults,
Moore! Start using your head

for more than just a paperweight
for your body. Paquette!

You've got the largest helmet in
NATO, I'd rather have your

head full of nickels than a
thousand dollars.

Warrant Officer mustachio,
waxed pitchfork tines,

the brine of our sweat, days
without sleep,

bus station goodbyes on
my way to Gagetown.

Officer Candidate lost his
meal card. Standing awkward

in front of the Warrant, Sasha
asked for a new one. *No problem*

Officer Canada, I'll requisition it.
Next day, meal card number

painted on tractor tire
that Sasha had to push.

High explosives, M67 grenades,
machine guns and tirades

from our CO who wanted
to know where we'd been,

rifle drill and bayonets, returning
salutes from privates,

the only folks I outranked for
two years, extra duties,

a stick in the eyeball that popped
on night patrol, another maiming,

I don't have any war stories
just ones from training.

FLAK JACKET
for Shayne Henry

It was more like a flak jacket
than a life vest,

swells with ghostly spines,
rising and dying.

Drunken crewman left him in
The Northumberland Strait

staring up; the blinding brass sunset
tuning for a second line.

Almost to Pointe-du-Chene wharf
when they declared *Man Overboard,*

the moon, a lucent trumpeter's
cheek,

one pin-prick shore light
flickering like a votive candle,

an improbable swim-distance
across a saltwater desert.

Jelly fish scourged, friction welts
laughing on his sides,

he prayed, it became a metronome,
Our Father—stroke—glide,

who art—stroke—glide,
in Heaven—stroke—glide.

By midnight the moon was reading
over his shoulder;

imagining his funerary dirge when
feet found sand, stumbling rock,

eyes swollen shut, elbowed and kneed,
cried out.

Lady Wisdom's airy voice asked,
Are you the one they're searching for?

Threadbare when he crawled ashore;
we all are; temporary, with or without

the hope that can keep us swimming
long after our bodies fail.

May your life-preserver be
a divine flak jacket,

deflecting serpentine tongues, tridents,
hollow horns;

every soul is touched and tested,
forehead stapled, crown of thorns;

endure the lonely pain;
atone for your sins,

do stay afloat,
do–si–dos with dorsal fins.

The Canonization of Stan Rogers

Tin cups of moonshine smell
like bandages,

alcohol alchemy, transubstantiated mash
causes drinkers to shudder;

baritone voices, kitchen songs, mud in
your eye, here's to your mudder.

Thrashing bluefin rise like harbour ghosts
between Starling Island and Hart Rock,

where lobster boats bait, drop their traps
between ancestral shipwrecks,

inland, giant turbines stand as tall
as Saint Stan;

shrouded by a fog that pulses from
Chedabucto Bay,

someone unplug those fans, they're
blowin' in a white squall.

Suspicious shorebird perched high
above the mainstage mast,

a maidenhead, listening;
an angel on overwatch.

Canonization requires two verifiable
miracles,

like stigmata, statues bleeding, a
Madonna weeping leaf lard tears:

so few are the mosquitoes in Canso
this night, and—

everyone knows the chorus
to Barrett's Privateers.

DRIVER'S TEST

Scheduled for Friday afternoon. A car liberates,
pulls us toward the horizon's setting sun.

He picked bouquets of clumsy words for the girl,
for years on the walk home down Academy Avenue,

the prospect of pulling up in a Malibu
made him sure-footed, steady enough to take a chance.

In the most matter-of-fact manufactured moment
he asked her out for Friday night. Saw their lives

arcing synchronously, radiant as choir song,
together on a Chevrolet bench seat, odometer

clicking mileage over landscapes. He'd glide into
her driveway seeing the worthy house they would

build together someday. That evening, standing
in the porchlight alone, as if on life's stage without lines,

meeting her father, smiling through shame, car idling,
his mother at the wheel.

Hot Spoons

Sure, for measuring time, for diffusing
sugar in slow clockwise circles,

as if winding an odometer backward,
pull it out steaming, then press smooth

steel heel against unsuspecting wrist.
The jolt and jerk response impossible

to deny, we pull away from pain,
all of us, sometimes knocking an elbow

against a chair, causing some type of
collateral chaos.

The last time, at The Egg and I
truck stop off Highway 2, a gallery

series of egg paintings adorning walls,
he stung me with the hot spoon.

My arm shot out unconsciously,
struck the server's thigh

causing her to jump, my father
to chuckle, me to apologize,

smoldering in a flush of embarrassment.
His love was like that,

the electric jolt of pain within
the slipstream of our days.

THE LAST TREATMENT

Corresponding by thumbs
in the middle of the night.
Stayed up for a few hours.
Finley woke me
just in time to miss the bus.
Spill a coffee on my front seat.
Drop him off at school.
Roll in—hair messy and
I'm wearing a Grateful
Dead T-shirt. Go to class.
A kid drops
has a twelve-minute seizure.
Give a couple killer lessons
on semantic search engines
and algorithms,
the massive reach of troll
farms, and the online
misinformation echo
chamber.

I go over safety protocols
with my new scholars.
Fire exit, where to meet
on the rugby pitch
if we must leave school
for an emergency, we do
"Lockdown Procedure".
I tell them, forget everything
they have learned or heard
about lockdown procedure.
In my room, there is only one
procedure. "You are to
surround me with your bodies—
keep me safe." I say,
"There are many students,
but only one Mr. Moore."

Donnie the Brave

Three bottles of wine
for the gale
that came ripping our sails,
eavestrough strapping
peeled
from the house in sheaves,
a hangnail tin gutter—a
slashing ribbon
in the wind, carving her
initials
into everything, reaching
blindly,
the car's hood was a good
shield,
ornamented with gashes.

Donnie,
our trusted neighbour,
courageous messenger,
ran the Kraken's tentacled
gauntlet.
dressed like a North Sea
fisherman—
gave warning.
We armed ourselves with
baseball mitt,
hammer, and spike;
stagger stepped against
the sideways wind and rain.
When the Kraken flailed, I
palm-caught
its writhing tentacle,
stinging knuckleball.

We shouldered the twisting
alien limb,
while she shrieked, surged,
lifted
us off our feet, when, for
an instant
pinned to deck, Donnie
didn't hesitate,
brought hammer down
true,
and crucified it.
Releasing,
the great sea beast
shed her wounded limb,
bubbled away to depths,
unsatisfied.

Fireside,
all three corks were pulled,
having beaten back the
under lurker, staring
into flickering light,
glowing warm,
knowing the uncertainty of
wine dark seas,
in the lee side of the storm.

MY GRAVE MARKER

In this boneyard, asleep
'neath the cedars,

stars spin above, virtuous
headstone readers.

Enjoy your brief squint of time,
a toast to your warm souls,

share a dram of fine whiskey,
down through the wormholes.

Acknowledgments

Cheers to my friends at Harrison Trimble and Crandall University, to Professor Bob Spree, Coach Wayne Hager, Dr. Douglas Mantz, and Mr. Jason MacPhail. You influenced the arc of my life, are my teachers, and my dear friends.

My heartfelt appreciation to Terri Beckwith and Emily Loewen (aka E-Lo) for editing early versions of this manuscript.

Thanks to Chris Needham and NON Publishing for their steady hand. My hat is off to Andrew Lafleche for his early edit work on some of these poems from my chapbook *Trigger Fingers*.

Handsome Mark Sampson! Thank you—for everything. Thank you for editing work, mentorship, encouragement, and brotherhood. *Saint Stan forever.*

Corrine and Finley, you are my worthy pillars, who remind me what is right, true, beautiful, and good. I love you for it.